Journey

Laurie Brady

Journey

Journey
ISBN 978 1 76109 674 7
Copyright © text Laurie Brady 2024

First published 2024 by
Ginninderra Press
PO Box 3461 Port Adelaide 5015
www.ginninderrapress.com.au

Contents

1992–1994

Retrospect for Heroes	11
Fortieth Birthday Party	12
After a Brother's Death	13
Love's Done	14
Kiama Drownings	15
World Weary	18
Beauty Pageant	19
Inevitability	20
Passing By	21
Insensibility	22
Approaching Dural Squash Courts	23
And Feeling Will Be There	24
You	25
The Petty Pace	26
Moving House	27
Vicarious Experience	28
Waikiki	29

1995–1999

Horatio	33
Dreams	35
Airport Departure	37
Beyond	38
The Old Backyard	40
Revisiting	41
Donegal	43
Bob's Retirement	45
Penelope's Complaint	46
Old Soldier	48
A Love Song	49

Reflection	51
Reunion	52
On Death	54
Irish Setter on a Beach	55
A Prayer	56
Seduction	57

2000–2004

Father's Death	61
Glowing From His Morning's Shower	63
Indignity	65
Woman	66
Affair	67
Love Letters	68
Sex	69
Uncle Laurie	71
Road	72
Romance. A Sonnet	73

2005–2009

Another Life	77
Illusion	78
Dying	79
Acquiescence	80
Privet Moon	81
Crematorium	82
My Retirement	84
Waiting Room	86
Schooling	88
Recreation	90
Worship	92
My Room	94
Fathers' Day	95

2010–2013

Signs	99
Teachers' Graduation	100
To Peter	102
Signature	104
Love in General	106
Mad Susan	108
Henry Kendall Finale	110
Roads Not Taken	112
Liberating Love	114
St Dunstan's	115
Ultimate News	117
Memory	119
Rummy	121
Mr Lodge	123
Cotswolds 1	125
Cotswolds 2	126
Homage	127
Police Station	128
Old Mates	130
Neighbours	131
Little Things	133

2014–2016

Recall	137
Paternity	139
Surreal	141
Dementia	143
Unity	145
Twilight	146
Son	148
Comedian	150

Rhea	152
School	154
Reaction	156
Age	158
Wally	160
Transience	162
Death	164
Prospect	166
Uncle	168
Theatre	170
Regret	172
Time	174
Schadenfreude	176
Visit	178
Introspection	180
Egocentrism	182
Exit	184

1992–1994

Retrospect for Heroes

i remember your win at chess,
all hail the conquering hero,
with your modest claims of luck
and beaming face…
and as bearer of gifts,
with eyes reactive to our delights
and moist with love.
you'd even wear your pain,
a focus of infectious sense
that left us helpless
like ants in a storm.
it's not the literal years
of your age
and the crimping of flesh
that disturb me now,
but the look of submission
in defeated eyes,
the mute recognition
that this is the twilight time
between life and death,
the glaucoma of mind
and of spirit,
and retrospect for heroes.

Fortieth Birthday Party

avid minds not wholly impartial
judge the work of twenty years,
filing data on jellying flesh
and hair that's left to grey

nostalgia inspires the familiar tales,
a ritual of reassurance,
and memories of more impassioned days
recede with hazelnut torte

from collective déjà vu, happy birthday
crackles like a bad reception,
is cheered by hip hoorays
and champagne's foam in crystal

repartee out-clichés speech
and when the cake is cut
the toast to forty more
lulls the festive mood

beyond the window years away
the barking of a dog
and Aunt Gladys twists a serviette
in bony fingers

After a Brother's Death

it seems our lasting record of the dead
is often just a masquerade,
lunatic grins are all that's left behind,
stilted in a million family albums,
but you ignored convention's need
for smiling masks, and even when a photograph
was done, your face remained
impassively the same.

and when i look at snapshots of myself,
an elastic hanging grin between my ears,
i imagine the biting judgement of my heirs,
laughing at my shirt or tie or hair,
remarking what my face revealed of me…
since i still have time to choose,
which option should i take…
indifference or inanity.

Love's Done

she laughed at mustn't and did her want,
while lambent, raven, pink
and all the world applauded,
coaxing with a wink.

she smiled at shouldn't and did her must,
with contours warm and firm,
for love's requited joys shone bright,
and beauty had its term.

she mused at ought and did her could,
in mists of year and day,
the season's must her soon did make
chalky, sallow, grey.

she thought of might and did perhaps,
though leathered, chafing, cold
joy's promise now was unfulfilled,
time's legacy foretold.

she nothing laughed and wanted do,
but sap, nor blood nor sun
mustn't shouldn't couldn't did,
love's done was now begun.

Kiama Drownings

volcanic black rock like coral
is jagged and sharp,
and the ocean leeches the coast
with shattered white gore…
prehistory's landscape of reptiles
in three-tone grey.

tourists scoot like crabs
across the rocks
to peer at the naked sea,
and their own raw souls.
'it makes you feel so small',
the rare disclosing moments
as nature flirts.

a howl is chewed by wind,
and heads like corks
now bob on the ocean's belly
beyond the point,
beyond the stricken sister
bent in juvenile shriek.

a trawler lists in the swell,
slow motion silent,
staining the sky in dirtier grey
with visible chugs.
tomorrow the paper confirms an image
of bearded fishermen heroes,
salt of the sea and earth,
'we've lived here all our lives',
weather-mugged and forever awed.

oblivious
tourists buy their spoons,
their cameras fixing time
that won't relent its flow
beyond the point.

returning with bucket and rod,
a fisherman tells and swears,
a florid torrent of blame…
or pain for the folly of man
and a new unwanted claim.

the reception isn't right…
the sound is muffled
like a maddened heart,
the picture floats in wool,
and the trawler circles inwards,
leaning against the wind.

beyond the drama
the prologue stuns,
as bodies are raised
from the trawler's deck.
tourists press and crane,
regaling a need,
'children you say',
'the mother as well',
'if i'd lost one of mine…'

and the ocean leeches the coast
with shattered white gore…
prehistory's landscape of reptiles
in three-tone grey.

World Weary

as he watched the silhouette of gums
scribbling on the moon washed ceiling,
muted pictures formed and hovered
waiting for translation,
shadows on the edge of thought.
he saw some children years away,
glossy cheeked with spanking new perceptions,
rooting through the relics of his life,
tossing from the attic chest of flotsam
the warped and stringless racquet,
the curious books and ancient photographs.
it all seemed so familiar…
the brittle artefacts of lives
in endless repetition.
then a stirring in the bed,
a change of breath, a toast-sweet thigh,
as colour drenched the struggling grey
with floods of roasting light.
and on the gum tree's branch
a lorikeet, brilliant in armorial flame,
unlike anything he'd ever seen.

Beauty Pageant

herded in the wings to hear her number called,
she gazed with timeless eyes
as through familiar wooden slats,
and pawed at earthless ground
until her turn.
then with coquettish toss of hair,
she strode into the blinding lights and noise
with deftly jouncing female parts
and saccharine-studied smile,
rehearsed resilience in her stride
for those whose ogling stews fantasies,
but quantify her attributes of shape and line.
then from centre stage an expectant hush,
parading is complete, a question put,
and in the close-up camera frame
a captivating look, both charming and sincere,
as gently drawing breath, she lifts her head,
and moos.

Inevitability

grub-like and flaccid it shrinks
in his groin,
framed by hospital stripe pyjamas,
this pap that once saluted generation
half a life ago.
he brings the bottle nearer,
wobbling in a feeble hand
and draws the sheet.
many times i used to watch
as he hurried naked from the shower,
his manhood thick and long,
and marvel at my pristine pink.
now the talk's of getting well,
and repertoire of work and sport
seems out of place in such a dislocation.
we say goodbye
avoiding brittle reassurance.
a doleful wave,
ammonia bites and loiters,
and i mourn
a man and a world,
for all of us are issue
of passionate days
before a life retracts.

Passing By

as twilight bleached the day
of colour and constraint,
i saw a couple lying in the sand.
beneath a sky still daubed with red,
they moved as one in antique show,
a crass production, cast of two,
lit dimly by a watery rose
and orchestrated by the waves.
i had to pass close by,
intruding in a private world,
and feeling like the one
who'd been found out,
embarrassed and resentful.
a creamy moon had mounted from the sea
and watched indifferent to discretion.
a thigh emerged and snakelike curled,
lambent in the dying light.
without a sound i passed unseen,
forlorn
beneath a billion rising stars.

Insensibility

the moment you died
i must have been mowing the lawn,
at ten when the grass greened
free from the whiskers of frost,
then tickled the nose
with its sweet cut mash

the news came by phone,
sedative, matter of fact,
'an accident, he suffered no pain',
and the grocery list of detail
that in weeks to come
i would parrot as therapy.

for months i'd escape
to the porch at night
and look
to my Sunday school heaven
at the formless treetops
and restive wind that tossed
like a will-o'-the wisp
your elusive Sunday school spirit.

five years on and the clutter
has barnacled life,
the children's dental work,
commercial bills to be rolled…
my healing skin of glossy pink
is becoming a calloused hide,
and unreality takes another form
as dream eclipses dream.

Approaching Dural Squash Courts

the sounds of vigour surge and ebb,
the thwack of ball and clash of weights
that muscle fat and tighten abdomens
made doughy by roast beef and cabernet.
emerging tracksuit fit, elastic shod,
a couple, arm in sweaty arm.
across the road the graves
afford a meagre local history.
no faddish monuments of clinker brick,
but timeless marble tablets,
prideless upright in their river pebble beds…
and jam jars' tenth-real plastic flowers.
the juicy winds of spring are greening
where we walk, my son and i,
in sunshine's brilliant sporting whites.
while waiting for our game,
and squinting in the light,
we read the ancient epitaphs.
a fitting context i decide for one
of life's great lessons he'll recall
when i am gone, but what to say…
suspended here between two worlds,
the deep and trite find balance,
does anything suffice?
then from my side an eager voice –
'we only have five minutes now.'
perhaps he is the wiser after all.

And Feeling Will Be There

in my final bedridden days
i'll think of a storm
in wild bush heart,
with bent and screeching trees
in unrelenting rain,
and i'll be there,
with arms raised skywards,
not in a Lear-like
stance of madness,
but triumphant,
exhorting the rain
to needle and drench,
to mat and shine.
and when my moment comes,
i'll lie in a shallow watercourse
all slippery with water and moss,
a hard procrustean bed
of running ice
that bends me
to its elemental flow…
and feeling will be there.

You

gazing out to sea, i'd watch
the dimming eye of sunset watching me,
and think of you.
and when my tireless stare no longer was
returned,
i'd look in hope that you
might peep beneath horizon's blind
and call my name.

or escaping to the yard at night
the invited sentience of the bush
would bring you near,
and struggling in the feeling black
thick with jasmine and cricket's noise
my senses would compete
for sight touch sound of you.

and now that you are here,
melody of laughter, tug of flesh,
no distant focus or feeling sense
but solid beyond the fancy of mind's eye,
i wonder if the reality of you
is less than my imaginings.

The Petty Pace

it's not so much
the strutting and fretting
that we remember
but simple things
like the diosma bush
that grew across
the backyard cricket pitch,
the hallway carpet
thinning with footprints
to the bedroom door,
or the explosion
of chocolate scent
from father's weekend surprise.
perhaps a ginger taste,
a disarming look
or Rubens' head of a negro
bought as a print
with ice creams
from some bucolic store
to hang beside
the pantry door,
and reminding by
its humble strength
from ageless acceptance
that in the end
it's not so much
the strutting and fretting.

Moving House

once outside, the furniture seems to change,
crossing the line to contextual void.
bleached of sentiment it becomes the stuff
of inventories, respectfully prepared by Abbco Removals.
confederate of my own lobotomy, i watch my memory
removed by silent men in overalls…
and when they've gone, i walk the empty rooms,
all unhinged silence like a ghost town bar.
my bedroom chrysalis is empty of the books
that surrounded me with answers
in my greener question seeking days.
and still the pittosporum taps the pane
with nutty fingers, aching with my old projections.
i take one final look and imagine
my room a month from now…
a nursery bathed in sunlight yellow
and cottage collection print…
or a study in masculine flock
with thick fur rugs and Boer swords.
my mother continues to clean, swabbing away
the residue of lingering memories
lest they be left like spirits
without a benediction.

Vicarious Experience

gentle country town
with a clutch of homes,
a snatch of cattle dogs
and a general store,
collapsing beside a jacaranda
which lifts the concrete kerb
it carpets in fibrous lilac.
all that's painted flakes
except the Pepsi Cola sign,
offensively modern.

on a floor of hewn planks
i peer through counter lolly jars,
am greeted by a round and ruddy face,
moistly Dickens.

returning to the car
i recreate this merchant's day
from hearty sausage breakfast,
the tortoise pace of daily trade
and evenings with a wife
i reckon fair and plump.

and so i've known the lives
of postal clerks and fishermen
and shop attendants everywhere,
i've been there with them all,
a fellowship of sense
concealed behind a thousand
bland perspiring faces.

Waikiki

this transplant corso from the Gold Coast
has another name. the impression is the same.
postcard beach slots in to high-rise,
glass to glass.
bethonged and not yet leisure-teethed,
the family ambles, tourist rubber-stamped.
along a beach front, bodies bloat in sand,
and cellulite spreads like measles
pitting roasted thighs.
children castle-mark their territory,
contesting claims in yankee drawl,
and swarming among the vendors
of surfing lessons and sailboat rides,
cameras tote the Japanese tourist.
approaching between the gleaming rickshaws
a handsome Hawaiian woman, festooned with flowers,
places a scented lei around my neck…
and speaks of her son's tuition fees.
beyond a passing interest in a brilliant green macaw,
and souvenir shell trinket stall,
i read the sign. 'Baskin and Robbins,
Thirty-one Flavours.'
is this why we've come five thousand miles?
i avoid the usual litany of denial.
after all i'm no philistine. perhaps
i'll discover paradise in
rainbow sorbet and Florida blueberry.

1995–1999

Horatio

it's you i admire, Horatio…
when the Hamlets of the world
all bleat about injustice
and rail against a sea
of troubles,
you seem to understand.
is it really a noble heart
that abuses a simple mother
or sends a blameless Ophelia
to her death
insane with grief.
your own soliloquy might deplore
the oppressor's wrong,
the insolence of office
and pangs of despised love,
but you don't wear
such slings and arrows
upon your sleeve,
ranting and wreaking havoc
wherever you go…
and yet you're always there,
not one to steal a scene,
for wisdom is upstaged
by hate and rage,
but loving and aware.

so i'll be there like you
at a thousand different ends
of purposes mistook
and accidental judgements,
providing a shoulder,
a politic word,
or a brief for Fortinbras.

Dreams

i think you're obsessed she said
i'm not i replied
but you're always dreaming of boats she complained
and tossed back her hair
i've seen you at night she wouldn't relent
you're leaning against the rail
with your hair blown sleek in the wind
and it isn't a porch with hydrangeas around
but a boat in the sea
with the roar in the sails when you heel
and the spray blowing needles to ginger your face
i sometimes think
that you want to escape
and i contemplate dousing your dreams
with a bucket of ice-crusted water
and would
but it might be more real

you made love tonight she resumed
but i know your heart wasn't there
i'll bet it's the sailing again
so how do you think i should feel
when a boat you can only invent in your mind
is your passion
i don't think that's true i replied
but i really believe she began
and her words were lost in a sigh

so nothing was said for a week
till she came as i read
with an interrogative look
that beckoned response
and a purplish and pink hydrangea
gripped by the stem
this boat of your dreams she began
do you think i could sail
we could both get away
beyond the bitter sweet moon

before very long she was hooded and dressed
the windcheater zipped to a delicate throat
and her cheeks were agloss
like an apple that's waxed for a sale
she leant on my arm and buffeted wind
as she tugged at the wheel
and steered the front porch
by the stars

Airport Departure

the airport has a space age view
of jigsaw grey and fading blue,
a place of steel and tar
where buildings glide on wheels
and planes mope home
like scolded dogs
with noses to the scent.
the waiting people doze
or read alone,
and families chat till cliché-spent,
their thoughts attenuate like fairy breath
to vague tomorrows.
then surging down the chute
with last goodbyes,
beyond emotion's press
and sage advice
they disappear to silence.
alone in voiceless space
unique and frail,
the world mutates
to endless uncertainties,
and i await my flight…
and Godot.

Beyond

i remember his muscles
the colour of muscat
in sun
all lustred with sweat
as he worked on the fence
and the lyrical way he spoke
with total command

then when he returned
to astound us all
so spectrally thin and grey
with eyes retreating into his skull

it's grown so fast
Tamara whispered
cutting quiche for lunch
and Susan ran to hide
unless he see her tears

yet when i think of him
i also think of Dave
a rough and tumble Labrador
with velvet snout of grey
that took the sapless arm
so gently in his mouth
i swear they walked with one intent
to sit pressed close
beneath the turpentine
and looked towards the hills

they've both gone now
and yet i often wonder
what it was they saw
together felt
beyond the summer haze

The Old Backyard

my father planted a tree
on the cricket pitch
in the old backyard
as if it wasn't hard enough
to bowl around the hedge
at a brother defending the fruit box
with naked shins and a paling bat

i grew up there
observing my father plant new rhubarb plots
by thrashing the turf against his spade
to free the rich grained earth
and bloated worms

it's where i fed the chooks
that scavenged in their filth
beneath the mulberry tree
to pick at seed in purple fruit

i never liked the chooks
that huddled to watch with primordial stare
or scuttled away on claws
of natal red
to leave the fragile warm mementoes
of their sex

tweaked by wooden pegs
my mother's undies
fluttered on the hoist
mysterious satin sacks
ballooning in the wind

Revisiting

i walk among the goitred weeds
and leaves
that strew the tennis court.
the loam is baked
and lifts like scabs,
a net post leans awry.

i used to play at night
when gums and turpentines
were charcoal green
and luminous
in shafts of drenching light
that teemed with motes,
when this became
a theatre in the round,
a swathe of brilliance
in the dark.

i play pretending strokes,
the spinning second serve,
a backhand slice
i follow to the net
in coat
and patent leather shoes
that shatter tinder leaves,
and crumble cakes of loam.

a dog begins to bark
reverberating through the years,
and Archie
shrivelling on the vine-choked porch
next door,
delays the lighting of his pipe
to catch my eye
and nod.

Donegal

we have an irish setter
and Donegal is his name
he's big and rough and gangling
we love him just the same

he'd steal meat from the butchers
and scavenge at the store
he'd bring home neighbour's chickens
he ate the garage door

he'd run through school assemblies
or through the local church
he'd disappear for ages
and spark a family search

they say you cannot train them
i strongly disagree
he went to special classes
the change is there to see

he does the children's homework
and cooks their evening meal
he drives them to their parties
knows exactly what they feel

he earned a rare exemption
to do a law degree
he'd catch the train to uni
and never pay the fee

a bachelor's with honours
was a first throughout the land
he went to graduation
to shake the governor's hand

but striding on the platform
with trencher in his paw
he felt the call of nature
as he'd never felt before

and forgetting he was upright
began to lift his leg
went crashing through the lectern
and sprayed the governor's head

Bob's Retirement

jocular contented Bob, source of endless good cheer,
greets his guests with the personal touch,
and strains to be witty. sixty surround the tables
where sugar stickies the creases from overstuffed mouths.
some are there to be seen. for others it betters
the plastic lunchbox taste of rissole sandwiches.
rattle of spoon and glass school bells formality.
'it's forty years since Bob began' – the recipe old
as that for scones: the shallow history,
the would-be funny retirement quotes, 'but seriously though.'
thoughts commute in time, ego-involved…
many are standing with Bob, shifting weight in modest receipt
of compliments, thinking what words could capture their life,
what parting insight might squeeze a tear.
the women fairy clap, juggling cups of tea.
the conventional gift unnerves, the tangible end,
and retreat to expected jest as Bob replies
dulls to catalogue of thanks, 'and Eunice most of all.'
younger colleagues contemplate the match, the other life
begetting children, the recompense of growing old.
applause and 'very nices' signify the end.
goodwill handshakes, a kiss from those who dare presume,
and the room is as bare as the ladies' plates.
five minutes have gone, and the speechmaker, spry,
sighs with relief, and returning a meaningful glance,
'thank God he's gone, now we'll get something done.'

Penelope's Complaint

not married twelve months and Ulysses is gone
to fight in the trojan war
and i'm left to rear Telemachus alone
and be badgered by suitors galore

and who fights a war for twenty-odd years
though Troy is certainly far
to not send a single missive or gift
let alone have a week's R and R

it isn't much fun to weave every day
and unravel it all by night
while Ulysses is always out with the boys
it really doesn't feel right

i'm tiring of thread and my hairs half grey
you'd think i'd the patience of Job
but the people of Ithaca think i'm a dolt
to spend twenty years on a robe

it's a funeral hood for my father-in-law
old Laertes will give it full use
but unless my Ulysses returns home soon
i'll lose this only excuse

i've needed support for such a long time
Telemachus now eats like a horse
poor Argus needs bones and a gentle walk
and then there's the garden of course

i'll draw up a list of the suitors today
my battered heart no longer sings
that no good selfish calculating user and lowlife father and mate
who else can shoot arrows through rings

Old Soldier

it isn't only pride that makes him march
on tinder legs with brittle gait,
and yet he needs this stoking day
of highland bands,
and wide-eyed children waving plastic flags,
who'll later want to know
how many men he killed,
and if he fought with Claude van Damme.
the clapping crowd behind the barricades,
sustained by Coke and chips
and gentle gratitude,
can't read in cataract eyes of grey
the terrors of fertile night.
perhaps he'll later end his pilgrimage
with ancient friends
in one of Sydney's pubs,
where pain and mirth are volatile
and pitch like two-up coin,
attenuating in the yarns that must be told,
and yearly toasts in tepid beer
to Sandy, Jock and mad dog Dave,
as proof that after fifty years
everything was real.

A Love Song

come with me
to a cliff that's sheer
where beyond the gleaming froth
the ocean belly is teal
and goosed by moon.
then shiver with me
and embrace the cold…
we'll reminisce,
and from the brittle artefacts
of time
we'll share elastic thought
and tender sense.

come with me
to a bed that cannot cloak intent
with feather down,
or hide what's real
beyond our yearning.
let's make sense of awe
and match what's fresh and sweet
with finite love,
the tug and rub of flesh,
the deep organic heat
and antique calm.

come with me
to all that's true
beyond desire,
and when you know the pain
and doubt,
recall a cliff that's sheer
and raw with cold
where feelings flared and burned,
and when we gave the more we had,
for both were infinite.

Reflection

i didn't know him well
but what i knew i liked.
the eulogy will say
that when they made poor Frank
they threw away the mould,
and then the over forties
all will sigh.

the gulls ejaculate
from scraps of bread and chips,
their nemesis a naked boy
whose penis hangs like plasticine
beneath a tumid belly.

i came for quiet
to contemplate my death
and hear the susurrating waves
or oboe sounds
from distant birds,
but not this squawking anguish
tearing at the sky,
and shrill of girls
who swim.

it seems there's never time
for any cast of thought
to colour resolution.

Reunion

it's like a cataract that silken moves
across the eyes
to blur recall
and sense,
a little change perhaps,
her figure lean,
though thick around the hips and arms,
the hair still blonde
at least in hotel light,
and eyes that flash the licence
of a child.

we hug,
a mandate of the missing years,
'you haven't changed at all' and
'let me see it must be
nearly twenty-seven twenty-eight…'
and then the thaw,
the barter of our separate lives
before the recollections melt
to mirth
and pleas of innocence,
'i never did',
'i never knew you felt that way.'

a plane to catch at 8 a.m.,
what now,
perhaps i'll make a politic retreat,
and walk along the beach
with trousers rolled…
the glow of sentiment
and latent sense
might fan to flame,
a close romantic meal,
a splash of candlelight on faces ruddy
from the swim of wine,
then afterwards…
emotion symbol portent recompense
or love
displaced by time.

On Death

my love is not the measure
of this departing hour
for our relationship burns on
beyond mere temporal death

there's comfort in the thought
that you're not really gone
and that your presence dwells
as sentience in the wind

perhaps you'll catch me soon
in the salad green of day
or the lucid hush before a storm
and whisper in the air

till then i cannot greet as friend
the pain that palls my sense
yet know that it must crack
the shell to spill my understanding

and so i'll feel my feelings
buffet my heart with anguish
conspire with you in wry asides
until surrender makes me free.

Irish Setter on a Beach

he bounds along the beach
with copper fur on fire
in setting sun,
his amber eyes aglow.
we laugh
to watch his meaty tongue
roll back and forth
like wipers on a car.
and as he nears us
thrilling to his verve
and calling out his name,
intent to capture and constrain,
embrace his freedom,
thieve his transient glee,
he swerves a pace away
to shower us in a veil of sand,
elusive as a moment's joy
and fugitive as time.

A Prayer

my God
who is just cause
for a world
that's beautiful and cruel,
should i presume to understand…
or shape my reason
to the procrustean bed
of faith.

and are my stylised prayers,
so hobbled
by feeble thought and word,
and offered on my knees
or in a waiting room or car,
already known,
my petitions a need you recognise
yet still demand.

have i been free
for all these years
pursuing selfish ends,
and seeking you in crisis,
or were you always there,
a part of me,
in silent prescience…
how much of me my God
is me,
how much is you.

Seduction

they sat on the lounge together
the music was soft and serene
a scenario for seduction
a familiar and age-old scene

i'm not well liked he confided
and tenderly held her hand
i know girls might find me attractive
if only they'd understand

he related all of his story
his malady as a boy
and the pain of adolescence
there'd been such little joy

she sat quite still as he prattled
and never uttered a word
but watched with eyes unaverted
he really had to be heard

an hour or so later he finished
the tears made his eyes half blind
she's just so delightful he realised
so patient and caring and kind

with coyness he fondled her shoulder
then circled her waist with his arm
she didn't resist his advances
and didn't show any alarm

so awkwardly reaching around her
and fumbling behind her back
he pulled quite hard at the fastener
releasing it with a snap

she collapsed in his arms atremble
with that same unerring stare
and a sound that was shrill and whirring
he'd bloody well let out the air.

2000–2004

Father's Death

the hospital called the day he died
and bid me come. a death however close
is always fired at point-blank range.

'palliative care' the door announced: a no hope synonym
beyond the maze of surreal corridors
where silent spectres drift between two worlds.

you enter, realise at last he'll never swing
those heavy doors, advance with buoyant tread
to sunlight's pretty, or even mundane things,

and always selfish, contemplate your own demise
right there, not where your final arrow lands;
what room or road awaits your programmed end.

'he waited till i came', the endless plainsong
of death, an incantation you'll soon recite
with growing faith and shrinking self.

he slept. a throat unable to swallow
elongated his open mouth. desultory chatter
flared and died like matches in the dark.

i didn't hear the modulation of his breath,
no final sigh or click, no guttural noise
from one who liked to steal a scene.

'i think he's gone': the end you knew would come
and half accept, yet even certain certainties
resist the slug of mugging fists.

there isn't much to say. a few disarming tears,
a reassuring platitude. you watch his spirit leave:
a sleight of hand that substitutes an effigy.

you act and watch your act, and ponder
if your kiss that pastes his greying cheek
might patronise, perhaps a compromise in death.

then from the windowpane you look for signs:
there is no picture blue, no sentient trees or wind;
it's strangely quiet beyond a radio's nasal drone.

Glowing From His Morning's Shower

glowing from his morning's shower
and the wattage of his smile,
mr. J bestows
an Eastwood multi-fronted red-brick kiss
on mrs J,
significant more for sentiment
than flowering peach
or last night's heavy dance of love; and
(being pattable)
pats the heads of Chloe, Fern and Tim
who biting into toast and reputations
don't say a thing.
then sunny mrs J
scrambles mothers' club and Wednesday tennis eggs
and then (unscrambling)
says it's three o' clock for Chloe's jazz; and
don't forget the bagels at the mall,
and by the way,
i did enjoy last night.

strewing clothes across three rooms,
a smug lubricious grin lay down with mr. J,
and not to mention mrs T
who footy club and blonde split-level checkout chick
believed it right to ask about the kids,
and beth of course;
whereon the shoulders of a mr J might well have drooped
if he'd been standing up
(and not so horizontally nude); and yet could still
assume his best 'she doesn't understand me look,
she's not like you.'

and so the reputation for 'compassion'
mrs T enjoyed was served
and mr J found solace
in the empathetic clench of hips

it being a month
mrs J (her whole world everyone all-the-time dress) unzips,
'my husband'll soon be home, let's make it quick.'

Indignity

when others see indignities
in tubes and plastic bags
that plumb
the inner residues,
and in some shuttered room
where gerberas tease the scent of death,
implore a sign
they know will never come
from eyes impervious
or lunatic in disbelief,
they think about their end.
beyond the clichés of a life
lived to the full,
the climax of a bold release,
i hesitate.
perhaps in years to come
there'll be a purpose for my impotence:
the bowels that run to swamp,
and silent words no laxative can free.
the reason may be mine,
an insight in the evensong of life,
or yours, a maxim in my narrative
of death.

Woman

the image of a woman's flawless gloss
i find devoid of lure. i'm at a loss

to understand why something that's so rare
and personal, albeit body hair,

the clad of blemished thigh, or print of line
is not regarded as a welcome sign

of something special, something wholly real
that grants a woman bold unique appeal.

yet still beyond the worship of a form
there's something more seductive than a warm

engaging voice, a titillating smile,
or manners that create a certain style,

the secret's understanding of her sex,
and how she might express it with finesse.

Affair

unwelcome morning sunlight throws a lemon rhomboid
on the bedroom wall.
she stretches feline on the bed
and rubs the soles of both soiled feet.
the scent of kippered morning-after
nags her memories of the night,
a play enacted in a multitude of beds:
the honeyed talk, the bumbling overture
that makes no pretence of finesse,
yet isn't worth the effort to resist,
conclusion's hurried march.
she acts so well: an artiste
in seduction's light and shade
who commentates beyond the script.
her men are faceless now and stuffed with straw,
their names are cold ascriptions of her disregard.
he'll ring today. she'll wait a day or two
before her curt reply.
it doesn't work for me she'll say.
it never does.

Love Letters

these ancient letters, annotations of a tender past
still speak to me. dormant in their piles,
their feeling reticent in rubber bands,
they have their sentient freedom once a year.
a woman pledging dire self-sacrifice,
the prosaic proof of burning love,
is now sequestered in a Mosman dining room
with Raoul. another written from a hospice bed
is signed 'forever yours'
as if i might entice her back to routine pain,
dissatisfied by small returns.
they might be some indemnity for age,
these fragile epitaphs to love,
or even blind conceit.
perhaps they should be posted yet again
and clearly marked with 'whereabouts unknown'.

Sex

that tacit stage in sex's hidden rush
had come, when prologue done,
they reached a point of no return.
a gravid pause when expectation peaks,
the readying of limbs for body's meld;
and then she gives a sudden start
to see him hurriedly remove his leg
and prop it up beside the bed.
a brief resistance follows fright
or just the unforeseen
but swells once more to urgent need.
supine again, she gestures with her arms
to welcome bold advance, but sees him
shed an arm, a shoulder, foot and eye.
'it's me you felt the urge to love,'
he reassures as she retreats,
protecting sudden private nakedness
with knees raised to her chin.
'that might be true,' she pouts, 'and yet
there's more of you upon the floor
than in the bed.'
'i'm just an object of your carnal need,' he bleats,
'it isn't really me you want, the quintessential me,
perhaps you need the beefcake at the gym;
i thought you were a class above.'

she soon relents, reclining gingerly upon the bed
with soft and mournful eyes
that even when she deftly frees her head
to place it on the dresser
near the bed,
observe his shock with sweet regard.

Uncle Laurie

not pert or even sweet at one,
all lobstered pink and pursed,
i never saw the smiles that won
her parents. two was worse;

grotesquely overweight. an age
to feel the world's rebuff;
a pother of racking howls and rage.
but three was enough

to forgive. from grub to butterfly
she took my hand, a balm
in autumn garden walks, and spry
in party dress and charm.

she told me secrets, laughed and bossed;
it promised so much more,
at least i loved before i lost:
she didn't live to four.

Road

along the road i met a guy
who asked for cash. so i can buy

my son some medicine he said
he has a tumour in his head

and giving him the change i had
he seemed obliged. i sure am glad

it's you i met. along this road
you must watch out for every mode

of killer, thief and saboteur
the pimp and cheat, philanderer

and then of course the hypocrite
i smiled and thanked him for the tip

some words of cheer about his son
and felt the barrel of his gun

Romance. A Sonnet

it's Bill. i wonder if you want a date.
i think you're hot! i hope it's not too late
to call, but Monday's when i have a beer
with all my mates, and if i'd tried to ring
there's all the noise of pubs, the guys would jeer
and hassle me, we wouldn't hear a thing.
Tuesday's training, Thursday's Kosta's fight,
i have to work my arse off Friday night.
so how is Wednesday? damn, but this is rare,
it's State of Origin, but you could come
and watch the game. the blokes will all be there
with stubbies, dressed in blue. it might be fun.
we'll all be ravenous when you arrive,
so could you stop and get Kentucky Fried.

2005–2009

Another Life

i've picked the memories clean
like pilling on a vest,
the holidays of dog-rich leisure
sprawling in the sun,
the pillow dreams embellished
after procreative sex,
our yeasting needs sedated,
cooled by thoughts of coming years
and august nights;
and then the children,
potpourri of years;
the baby smells of sweetened milk
to teenage Pleasures, Equipage apres rasage.
confederates
in the act of growing up
we shared our bodies,
kept our minds untenanted.
and now there's nothing left;
these relics of my former love
are stringless racquets,
closet's broken toys and headless dolls,
my feelings once ejected
like the trash in beachfront gutters
hold another focus now,
my leg locks with another's while i sleep,
and when the fickle shadow
scuds across her timeless question
settling on my pause,
she ushers in the sun.

Illusion

tonight the water's silver sheen
runs tapering towards the moon
to mirror hidden truths.
these scenes of beauty rousing latent sense
still resonate with melody of laugh,
and frame the doting looks
he recreates throughout the years,
the natural world a shrine
to test his loss
with bitter-sweet desire.
his wife has caught him unawares before,
her gentle call to dinner interrupting reveries
that soften poignancy
and warm his gratitude.
he knows forgiving time
that mellows heartache to a lived philosophy
has fashioned an ideal,
the angler's boast that grows with each report.
and so be baulks at thoughts
of seeing her again:
perhaps a little coarsened
by an ample life,
her puzzled look before recall,
and comic revelation of their private narrative
to entertain a husband's playfulness.
escaping from a meddling moon
to certain warmth inside,
his grand illusion's still intact,
a suspect martyrdom
that's safer than reality.

Dying

only hours ago i raised her
from the faecal scented bed
to hold her sapless in my arms,
a desiccated fallen branch,
a wire frame surrogate,
her will to die emancipating touch
she always thought a risk.
and now asleep at last,
she's waxen, silent, pillow-propped,
her chin too heavy for her mouth.
i kneel to speak the ritual words,
the talk no longer mediated by her kitchen bench,
the evensong of death,
an affirmation of her life,
permission to depart,
and yet i feel a fraud
dispensing schoolboys' toilet notes,
and strewing platitudes like trash,
a defrocked priest
who has no business with the intimate.
i pull the curtain round the bed,
defence against the broken snores
and ancient woman opposite
who sits with eyes screwed tightly shut
and fig soft legs agape.
a last goodbye
before my passage to the starless night
and sky that has no face,
that's more a sea than sea itself.

Acquiescence

she feels a rustling in the bed,
a subtle change of breath,
the tension she alone can sense
that signals need,
and then a heavy arm
as cumbrous as desire
collapses on her naked thigh.
there's no retreat or compromise,
no longer can she plead the virtue of a single girl,
defence from age-old male assault.
their sex is analgesic now,
and swallowed like a Panadol with tepid water
at the ensuite sink,
the act that might have stood for love
before it disappeared.
his final coaxing words
begin the pantomime,
and she unfurls from broken sleep,
supine and soft
against the edges
of his hard relentless need.
he moves to rhythms of his own,
indifferent to the opaque eyes
a breath below.
to acquiesce is better than to abdicate:
she's learnt that script by rote
but dare not speak her part.

Privet Moon

'and why was i the horse's rump',
a wistful smile
and vision of a snowy haired duet
enthralled with infant playground games,
or leaping from
the jasmine porch-cum-rocket ship
to privet shaded moons.
there's no mistake,
it's David Mills,
'donations to the cancer fund',
and hidden by my morning Telegraph
i contemplate my life,
removing chunks from history's edifice
like children's building blocks.
my energetic wife makes pancakes
for ipodded sons
inured from death writ large
by corpses piling high behind the television screen,
while ill-at-ease with recollection's claim
and destiny that made a simple choice,
i baulk at just a mote of ownership;
and each familiar name the years expel
is pause for fleeting thought,
until i make a safe retreat
to resurrect the blocks
or fly
to other privet moons.

Crematorium

for Gwen,
a touch of old-world charm
with just a hint of lichen,
dulling brass,
a contoured shrub and pared down roses
waiting for their time,
their scent and bloom capricious
in the face of death's fidelity.
the ancient women give affirming nods
to rectitude and taste,
their hair as blanched as summer cloud
and sparse as maidenhair:
'it's what she would have wanted, dear.'
i edge along the row of garden plaques
to metal tablet 24194
as if i'm treading on the faces of the dead.
so would she care,
compacted talcum in her metal box,
to lie beside a foreign sounding gent,
her sex now purified,
suggested only by a name.
the stuff of gossip's all around,
the accident and suicide,
and those who blushed unseen,
the soul-mate virgin aunt
who might have shared a Sunday afternoon.
at least there's not a supplicating angel here,
or cherubs that console.

a neighbourhood of dead away.
the slap of waking sprinklers
fan their manna to thirsting souls,
the watery tick of earthly time.

My Retirement

i watch their faces watching me,
the devotees of scenes,
admiring, fond and curious,
to ratify the impact
of the eulogy,
my deeds extolled
and yet i wonder if it captures
who i really am,
or can my soul be ever bared
by acts prescribed by protocols
and gelded of their deeply human touch.
i'm not beyond
my fleeting moment in the sun,
the pride that's mantled
by a show of modesty,
the hero's claim
that it was nothing after all,
and then the private recounts
of forgotten deeds,
insinuations of complicit acts,
the back slaps and the hugs,
the smudge of vinous kisses
gently tissued clean by caring hands.

tomorrow i'll return,
a lover to a moribund relationship,
i'll linger far too long to pack my things,
and mutter platitudes
that rattle like the marbles in a can,
and with best wishes cooling
from tonight's extinguished flame,
i'll make a dignified retreat.

Waiting Room

i watch
the rounded mouthings of the fish
that glide with goitred eyes
inside their phosphorescent world,
and wonder if her psyche screams
behind the door,
beyond the wadded stillness of the waiting room.
i sit beside a cheerless spray
of tenth-real flannel flowers
and thumb the scoops from dated magazines
on sex romps
tired romance and pregnancies,
while opposite
a drowning woman sinks a little further in herself
behind the vacant face
that's scourged to would-be rosy health,
a khaki envelope of scans unopened
on her lap,
their murky white and charcoal
mocked by Monet's *Poplars on the Epte*.
'are you OK' sounds subterranean,
a voice that i'm surprised to own
that draws a nod and silent thanks
beside the fish that hang in brilliant light.

the door unlatches noisily,
the specious safety of uncertainty
has gone, and in a timeless moment she'll emerge
behind a rush of bridled sense,
and i will know
before the merest tremble of a lip,
how fate that drives a wedge
between two worlds
adjudicates.

Schooling

the boys and girls were separate in our school,
in different buildings, with a yellow line
painted on the asphalt to define
the trusted practice of divide and rule.

along that line 'for boys' i had a race
against a girl with pigtails and a grin,
another spoke to me and for her sin
was taken to the mistress in disgrace.

the rules were etched in stone, immutable,
beyond the ken of children such as us,
we never questioned, never made a fuss
for adult sense was incontestable.

a flautist in a band of boys, we'd thrum
the march to class of children through the years,
'Do ye Ken John Peel' and 'British Grenadiers'
died agonising deaths to flute and drum.

a folkdance with the girls was soon prescribed
about a ritual circle on the ground,
and so the boys all moved to sound
of sixties static freely amplified.

what rare concession sanctioned touch as well,
it must have been a syllabus decree
to interact before our hormone's spree
consigned us all to heterosexual hell.

i'd meet my girlfriend at the schoolyard gate,
a clayton's bond just looking for a cause,
apart from lollies swapped in sweaty paws,
our 'love' was nominal, immaculate.

i do not think of freedoms won or lost,
the soul of culture changes through the years,
and rites of passage for our current peers
endure their own inimitable cost.

Recreation

it's silent when i enter bearing gifts;
a dozen sit and some incline,
all ringed by knots of walking sticks and frames,
and mantled from imagined draughts,
their faces vacuous as empty fields
or frozen in assent.
the television blues the weary grey
in faint narcotic haze,
yet no one looks or hears:
the only images are deeply private ones
with more repeats than sitcoms from the past,
unreadable in torpid eyes
that sink in lucent heads.
he's different,
even from a month ago,
retreat by stealth without the bugle call,
and somehow more submerged.
'how are you dad' reverberates,
a human spark that colours other eyes,
the rush of scent from dew-fresh jonquils
on the sill,
the sunbeam caught on frames of stainless steel.
he doesn't answer;
several others do,
and now the doorway frames a naked man,
perplexed,
his penis like a long-dead esmeralda rose
that's nested in some desiccated leaves.

the caustic blend of bleach and urine
trapped in shuttered rooms
might sweeten with the taste of butterscotch,
and so i share his gift,
dispensing sweets without a single thanks
to empty mouths that suck reflexively
and slow robotic hands.
perhaps it's all a blessing in disguise
to salve the sting of cruel ends,
a purgatory on earth,
or halfway house to blunt the sensibilities,
submitting half in love
with easeful death.

Worship

i put her on a pedestal
to worship love's true light
so all the people of the world
could share in my delight

i ordered marble on a base
a metre square and glossed
but couldn't even budge the stone
and felt my cause was lost

i needed something portable
that she could mount with haste
for theatres parks or garden walks
yet something rich in taste

then i could watch the people stare
indulge the odd aside
protect her from the envious
and bathe in lover's pride

that's why i made a podium
with steps for her ascent
complete with horns and flashing lights
to signal the event

because it was a bulky stand
a licence for the road
was designated 'pedestal'
but it collapsed when towed

that's when i found an old fruit box
stored underneath the stairs
she didn't like the label though
for Goulburn Valley Pears

she fell right through the rotten thing
and screamed obscenities
with torn and bloodied pantyhose
and skirt down round her knees

now still intent to show the world
that she's my heart and soul
i think i'll buy a trenching tool
and put her in a hole

My Room

short-term recollection wears
like fraying rope,
the longer term endures
unweathered by the years,
like thoughts of that first room,
my adolescent chrysalis
of bed and desk
and reassuring books
that harboured insights yet unknown,
where latent feelings simmered
in a stew of wild imaginings,
and all was portent in the world beyond:
the hale pittosporum's nutty fingers
thrumming on the panes
with schoolboy restiveness;
the television seeping blue
across the hall,
its canned hysterics mocking
bedside prayer;
the night sky bright and luminous
or pierced to tears
by interfering stars;
a young man's brimming feelings
keenly lived
before their enervation
by the sedative of time.
these memories mark the quest
of creeping age:
revisiting the past
and resurrecting passion lost.

Fathers' Day

we shuffle past the single occupant in number ten
who naked sits beside the bed; the wink of penis
shrinks beneath his scrotum, rugose, beige.
it's hot and fading blue outside; the warm earth
smells of springtime rain, and red camellias bloom;
angophoras tower beyond the fence; rosellas swoop.
my father lifts his arm, a roll of crepe around a stick
to point, perhaps salute. the birds alone excite him now.
the gifts we give bemuse, and so we unwrap those we bought
and must explain (it cannot be his frugal needs
have made us mean). from me, some sherry:
'have a drink with mum before your meal.'
we each take one of Lara's proxy sweets
and joke about the theft; i see the zephyr of a smile,
or was it just the dapple of the afternoon.
there's more i have to know, the history of our years
to set the record straight:
redemption, blessing, mateship, thanks.
it's all too late; perhaps he understands enough.
a shadow pulls the dozing day beneath our chins;
i know my partner waits at home, and feel a keen desire;
my body's gathered round my need, indomitable, hard.
'it's time for dinner, Dave,' a sister's there to help;
i wonder if his need is just as great as mine;
it's just as well that something beckons.
that and the birds.

2010–2013

Signs

no sudden mist of rain from violet clouds
for minds in avid search of signs,
although my drive away is metaphor,
consigning present loss to mellow past,
advancing by retreat.
at 3 a.m. the world's asleep
beneath a sky
that'd blushed by street light's amber stars
and cleansed by autumn chill,
and you are everywhere
to take your final leave,
the brief ubiquity
that's granted
when you kiss the cheek of time,
released at last from stertorous noise
and all ward three's disturbances.
and as the car glides noiselessly
on empty roads,
our dialogue's pure:
no need for secrets anymore
or all the checks of guardedness;
we're both at peace
and will not rage
against the dying of the light.

Teachers' Graduation

he hooks his gown and hood
behind the office door,
and swivels with his feet up on the desk,
to watch the swaying gum trees
drop pale-bellied leaves,
reviving the occasion's paradox
that everything remains the same,
yet won't stand still.
they come to strut the stage,
the rite of passage to a brave new world,
these fresh inheritors of promises,
cosmetic and assured,
their hugging dresses and their toothpaste smiles
that knotted feeling and desire,
and left him old as sandstone's fustiness,
and no more malleable.
the hall has emptied now,
and crumbs remain from sandwiches and cakes
where polystyrene cups glue coffee rings
on paper tablecloths.
his waxing testimonials from favoured students
segue to the master and apprentice photographs,
the softness of their shoulders
gentle still against his arm.

sometimes he's hugged or kissed,
and yet his 'let me know if i can…'
trails away,
for after all their world's too big an oyster now,
as out of context,
old allegiances will fade,
abetted by a problematic world
seductive with unleashed realities,
and heedless time.

To Peter

and i,
romance's bumbling hero
of an 1890s music hall,
aflutter near my heroine,
beneath a large membranous moon,
with such unease it had to breed calamity.
and so we shared our stories
of our first great loves,
we shy romantics with our actions stilled by fear,
and at a time when sex was sin,
yet made a natural claim.
as self-assurance now torments
the inhibition of those years,
we share our recollections sipping coffee,
flirting with the waitresses,
and hanging feelings out to dry.
i never will forget your fortieth
in fancy dress as keystone cops,
or when you slipped in mud to join the ducks,
your head emerging from the brackish lake
to make a plaintive 'quack';
and then that fated day
you took the blame for me and i for you,
to find another was at fault,
and knew that something special had evolved.

but are my many memories
just the same as yours,
or are some merely fiction
made more real when thinking makes it so;
or do they multiply,
embellished by the insights of our creeping years,
to fit the symbols that we now revere.

Signature

this pleasant man,
who looks like someone's neighbour
tending roses on a Sunday afternoon,
is now her lawyer,
keeper of expedience,
and splendid in a pin-stripe suit.

my errant fancy half-expected Dickens:
wooden benches in an airless room
abutting squalid alleyways,
an oil lamp coughing feeble light
and he an evil smelling Fagin
with a limp or tic.

beside me he assumes a camaraderie,
but Dior aftershave does little to appease,
and soapy fingers peel the pages,
pointing to the pencil cross,
Golgotha of a doomed relationship.

i'm there with her again;
the pouring of the slab in virgin bush,
the first unlocking of the door,
the creep to children's rooms
in awe to watch them sleep,
and dreams embellished late at night
and sealed with love and sex.

a gentle word reminds,
and as i take the pen,
the pointing finger (is it manicured?)
relaxes on the page;
perhaps he understands,
this hero of the Sunday rose,
and dealer in momentous wretchedness.

emerging from the granite and the glass
that muscles out the warm benignity of sky,
reality still lags.
has justice rendered me my due,
or have i just succumbed,
a victim of my self-belief
or life's caprice.

the carbon-scented air
is redolent with noiseless dreams.

Love in General

a spearmint scent invades
from father's stock surprise,
insinuating with my mother's lavender
and brother's fresh sawn wood and brine.
beyond the car side window
i initial my misted breath
the country hurtles by,
all open space beneath a pastel sky of baby blue
that smiles on straw green grasses
and a random jersey cow.
of course the metaphor is lost;
the world is far too big for nine-year-olds
to plumb its esoteric ways.
i watch my father's soft and long-lobed ears
that hang beside
the silver sprouting hairs around his neck,
and strangely wakened to his fallibility,
i feel a tenderness for all the world,
a feeling i'm too young to understand,
but when i leave the car
and its imposed complicities
to bicker with my brother's fractiousness
and query the injustices of adult law,
the feeling disappears.

yet even after all these years,
i'm often overcome by sentiment,
by small humilities i sense
in someone's look or act or words,
the all-absorbing gentle images
that bear the common longings
of a frail yet shared humanity.

Mad Susan

'so has he been today.'
she wheels her tiny luggage
to the corner that she owns,
her order just the same;
'mad Susan's table' the proprietor explains,
with literalness-cum-sobriquet.
the foreshore wattle mirrors gold
across the sunlit olive of the lake
where Susan claims a second patch,
to watch the ducks in gleaming phalanx,
and the sulphur-crested cockatoos play tag
between the towering gums.
'about so high',
she motions with a benedictory hand,
accosting kiosk passers-by.
'grey eyes and very regal,
possibly in khaki slacks and mustard top';
indulgent smiles invite the tale
they're loath to hear.
intrigued lunch customers enquire
and nod towards her lakeside seat;
'she hasn't missed a day in thirty years,'
the old proprietor relates,
'and always here,
the same old floppy hat,
umbrella all skew-whiff with broken spokes;
some feelings can't be numbed by time;
to keep believing blunts the loneliness.'

'tomorrow' Susan calls with cheer,
and all eyes turn towards her shambling gait,
and time stands still,
until the squeaking wheels are heard no more,
and silence for a moment overwhelms.

Henry Kendall Finale

are they prehistoric
all these water dragons warming on the stones
and symbolising passing time?
i watch from upstairs balcony
as silence shawls the inky hills
beneath an ecru light.
reptilian time that claimed my mother
smiles on children with insouciant goodbyes
that leave me gratefully alone.
i walk the soulless rooms a final time,
performer of my own lobotomy,
consigning family history to garbage bags,
or tagging it for Father Riley's store:
the bed dismantled
baring threaded mats of crumbling dust;
the ancient glass-topped dresser
crowded with emollients and bric-a-brac;
her wardrobe dead in sympathy,
to have its final rights
in St Augustine's clothing bin
with brassieres and blooming pants
i lift between my thumb and finger,
baulking at the intimate,
a son's uneasiness at hint of parent sex.

i'm tired and dirty now,
and find a wafer of her soap,
its perfumed subtlety no match
for bathroom's fruitcake heaviness,
and mindful of the allegory
i rinse her captured essence free,
her passing now complete,
and look towards the hills.

Roads Not Taken

the staffroom's my retreat,
escape from the miasma
of pubescent sweat and chalk.
at last i'm quite alone,
yet not beyond the muted voices raised in ire,
and cheerless student chants.
at twenty-three i'm virginal,
the lure of *Sons and Lovers*
tantalising me as much as them.
a knock, i turn, it's Ursula,
the name itself evokes romance,
exotic escapades,
this nascent woman in school uniform,
and carven,
nubile,
her hair that's shoulder-length and tousled blonde,
with eyes of quickening blue.
'you're the most loving man
i've ever known.'
Ursula, and still i mouth the name
with lingering vowels and sibilance.

a cliched narrative would cast her
with a reddening face,
and yet i'm sure that she was self-possessed
before she turned to go,
her frankness weening no embarrassment
and needing no apology:
and after all these years
it's one more lasting metaphor,
another line i might have crossed,
a further road not taken in the labyrinth,
the city of a million dreams
that lends no maps.

Liberating Love

tentative from shyness and uncertainty,
we walk beneath a canopy of sun-shot blue,
accompanied by percussive waves
and prating gulls,
our hands unlocking
for the script i finger scrawl,
the hard-wet letters bolder
in the displaced sand:
the subject 'i',
constrained but blossoming to generous 'o',
the symbol of inclusion and her sex,
to 'v' that plunges to a cusp of doubt
before determination's quick assent
and glide to 'e',
both opening and enshrining,
hurrying to 'you',
the other side of love beyond myself.

dismissing any portent
in the first obliterating wave
that smoothes the sand,
we cling to one another
like protective siblings in a storm,
in awe that everything has changed,
and all the waves and sands of time
can't weather such acknowledgement;
the rendered words
that free the guarded heart.

St Dunstan's

these chastening reminders of the dead,
subdue all visitors with certain prophecy:
both upright and askew,
or broken and face down,
a few have bold ascriptions,
prideful with corsage,
and still exert a claim on life;
while others smoothed by needling rain,
are lichened with their lost posterity.
the setting sun slants through majestic towers
to sharpen plots of sunlight
in the darkening shadow of the church,
as reverential,
stepping round the faces of the dead,
i read the epitaphs or let them speak to me,
these miserly chronologies
from which the flesh of life has atrophied.
the sun is now a peachy residue
that settles on the bottom of the sky,
and walls of rising sandstone chill the dusk.

i don't think Thomas Winthrop would oppose
my sitting on his tomb to share his peace,
the beauty and the silent consummation
of a thousand disparate lives,
but now it's time to go; the dead must get their rest;
the village postman
smarting with his Great War wounds,
the little girl with plague
 who never knew the secrets of her sex,
and Sarah Cavendish at ninety-three
who guards the church
she once adorned with flowers.

Ultimate News

composed at first,
he asks what needs be asked,
his calm as heavy as a summer eiderdown
that must be thrown aside.
the voice drones years away,
a blowfly circling on the light,
while numb he floats beyond himself to arbitrate,
as if he's not the sole agenda after all.

the sharing seems unreal,
his terror mantled by a show of common sense;
the sympathies of others volleyed
with avowals of enduring love;
his paranoia softened by nobility.
'i'll do this well.
i'll make my death
a crowning glory of my life.'

and then the fertile nights when sleep eludes
and paints perception black;
when demons nest in overactive minds
to mock the comfort
of his partner's sleeping breath
or toast-warm thigh,
and holograms of love ones
make their claims
with those who've gone before.

and so escaping barefoot to the patio,
and grateful for the ice of quarry tiles,
he sucks prodigious gulps of air,
the hunger for a life
that can't be stored for rainy days,
and searching in the sentient black,
he hesitates in wry belief that someone's there
with trumping rights
to overturn this mortal trick
and listen to his trembling plea,
before his silent bawl
implores a heedless world.

Memory

the Odeon is dark and hushed,
as aura-lit on stage
she sings in pure soprano,
head raised to the gods
and rarefied,
the whiteness of her throat exposed;
at ten i recognise what adults mean
by love.
the theatre's been a shopping mall
for half a life,
and yet the chastity of climbing notes
reverberates
for one nostalgic mind,
and keeps my fantasy inviolate.
i have no wish to contemplate
a harsh reality:
perhaps a hall of fetid children
in the grainy dark
with teachers on patrol,
my heroine anaemic in the light
and gangling in her tunic,
singing out of key;
and spare me from reunions
lest i find her with a face that's overripe
and backside like a shelf.

my memory is the only shield
against the killjoy of the passing years;
its preservation is a private trust,
the record of my history and identity,
and even proof of innocence,
that's somehow fuller
than experience.

Rummy

memories of the dinner table resonate
in dying fall,
the calls of kinship
fading with the truancies that time exacts.
the family ritual of after dinner cards
still scribbles on the mind
with looks like caricatures
or galleries of rogues:
my hostess aunt,
vanilla-scented and intent,
a slow release of steam in intermittent laugh;
her sister nonchalant
and brooding on more animated scenes;
the husband,
bland and tumid-eyed behind thick lens
who calls me 'son';
my father's studied pause
as if an intellect can govern chance;
my mother's eyes that nurse the world;
and opposite
a brother milky sweet yet serious.

they've all gone now,
and yet i cannot place myself
among the ghosts of ages past;
the images of me are counterfeit,
and forged anew
by evert foray of the mind,
in every increment of years.

who was it then that sat
with all the rest
in childhood innocence
before the whimsy of a shuffled deck.

Mr Lodge

the day is picture book,
with starting captions i provide;
the storm is only his,
the clouds already louring at the corner,
catching him in indecision's parody
before he scurries home.
'it's such a lovely day,'
the sister holds my gaze and shrugs,
'you're quite sure, Mr Lodge.'
and so we play gin rummy in the room
that shrinks with him,
stewed tea and ginger snaps instead;
our talk's desultory now,
for past has lost its way,
so why force challenges he dare not face,
or try to resurrect old dreams,
deflated like a party's sad balloon.
i'll recollect him swaddled in his bed,
the one immunity from fear,
with comfort in the things he knows:
elaborate cornices and frosted ceiling light,
the door that opens on his wandering thoughts
to capture muted voices from adjacent rooms,
familiar meals
and pills with prophylactic words at 8 a.m.
the sunlight squeezes motes through shuttered slats
to gladden orange gerberas wilting on the sill;
'so will i come again' i ask,
anticipating no encouragement.

he'll listen to my measured steps,
tick-tock receding on linoleum corridors,
until the welcome silence settles like a quilt.

Cotswolds 1

the dew retires from winking silver
as the sun climbs in the sky,
and in the understated light,
the golden symmetry of buttercups and bluebells
stipple verdant green.
i pick my way past hawthorn
and the steaming pats of horse's dung,
enlivened by the blackbird's song,
the efflorescence of the English countryside,
and look down on striated fields
with ancient houses sleeping in the town,
then something primal
makes me lie down in the field
among the smell and taste
of coaxing grass,
to stretch my limbs in dog-rich ease,
and look towards a pastel sky
that's seamed with threads of cloud.
and as the whole world opens
with the springtime flowers,
my cloistered needs evaporate in morning dew,
reducing me as no cathedral can.
is this where i belong,
supine for all eternity,
and gazing at the sun and stars,
as grass entwines me
and the saplings root me to the earth,
in welcome anonymity.

Cotswolds 2

alone,
i can't fulfil the licence
of the ancient kissing gates
that separate the fields,
and fancy is a lame alternative.
the ripened hills roll down in tussocks,
brightened by the English sun,
to meet my winding path
that's beaten flat by centuries of feet;
the scented air's alive with birdsong,
dun-nosed sheep stare foolishly,
and bees grow languid on the hollyhocks.
i cross a stile and stop,
to feel the silence settle like a quilt
that mutes the bleating of the sheep,
and warms my growing nakedness,
yet even when denuded,
stripped of past and future,
sanctified by this cathedral
of the natural world,
she's somehow closer than before.
so why choose now to reappear
when she's been gone so many years:
perhaps because i'm emptied
of myself,
or can it be that both of us
are closer now
to God.

Homage

if you are called to God
before i am,
i hope that time
won't carry on its heartless march
towards eternity,
but stop.

it isn't right
that all my thoughts of you
compete with all the scourges of a world
indifferent to your loss.
i have no problem now with time
that makes us grow and learn,
or even shrink infirm with age,
the glassy sands of time
that stop all things from taking place at once,
that help me through the years
to orchestrate the music in your laugh,
and see your eyelids flutter
when we love.

i only hope that thieving time
might deign to pause
when you are gone
and have the decency to weep with me
and pay you all the homage you deserve,
before i face the future quite alone
observing time rush heedlessly
to fill the past.

Police Station

imagine orange brick with fresh-pruned roses
patterned in the clay,
a modest sign in lettered black;
the rest escapes me now.
i know it was provincial,
and that country law is neat.
we must have looked diminished
standing at the counter,
robbed of presence,
atrophied in grief.
what did she think,
the pretty constable
whose eyes foreshadowed pettiness:
the neighbour's poisoned all our shrubs,
the cat's stuck in a pipe.
she waited, pen unholstered,
safety catch removed;
if only written words could undo what is done.
my brother i explain,
my parents mute beyond a useful sanity.
the thaw of closing winter's day
is in an instant palpable
in eyes that search my face
to glean life's lessons
from blood likenesses.

my mother takes the watch and sodden wallet
with a plaintive moan from shock revisited,
a harbinger of more;
but all continues spectral,
quiet,
the incantation's yet to come.
some things are just too big for words.

Old Mates

your passion hasn't gone;
it's simply mellowed by the buffers
life and time exact.
yet still our insights meet
from travelling different roads,
and from the ash of years,
ignite like embers,
lighting grateful faces in the gloom,
excited by the synergy.
and yet i ponder
questions i might ask to really understand
your journey here,
and how i might relate in word or act
my soul's desire,
so slippery now
and biddable like sun-dried sand.
we sip our coffee through the years,
and from your terrace
watch the swath of harbour glints
beyond the roofs
to stoke our wandering thoughts.
at times we muse
at what another twenty years might bring:
a fellowship of grace,
or full immersion in the dotage
of our separating lives.

Neighbours

nonagenarians holding hands
to watch the TV news
with all its fading salience,
and sinking in a high-backed lounge;
the widowed neighbours
relishing their new-found love,
with curfew every night at 8 p.m.,
unless of course his bowels protest
to make a quick retreat imperative.

they share their morning teas,
her slices still habitual fare,
incursions by their families
suspect challenges to growing ritual.
'so will i be with Herb,'
she asks the nurse who checks her bag,
'or Tom.'
placated by the answer
'heaven's not the same.'

do people know that final moment
when it comes,
and does life hurtle past
like gabble on a spinning wheel.
we found Herb on the bathroom floor;
he never could shed light.
her own demise a fortnight on,
was just as unassuming as her life.

authenticated by the half-real truths
of sepsis fibrillation cardiac arrest.
at least she foiled the age-old curse
of dimming time:
to beckon death that will not come.

Little Things

i'm grateful now for little things:
the magpies' a cappella
in the scented blue of spring;
the laughing dogs cavorting in the park,
these friendly epicureans
beyond the spoiling metaphysics of a life;
the old gent relic of a dying breed
who doffs his hat in passing by;
the long-deferred appeasing drink
to watch the tangerine
turn primrose on the bay;
but most of all,
the times i catch you watching me,
so reminiscent of the past,
when feeling laced with curiosity
was struggling to define itself,
a look now glowing from a face
that's settled
with a gently creased benevolence,
emotion mellowed
by a bedrock certainty.

2014–2016

Recall

she'd been his lover once. the eyes
of indigo give her away;
those eyes that ushered in the day
for months; the rest could be disguise;

as thickened by childbearing years,
face fluted by the captious light
of sun, she's heedless of the sight
her dowdy clothes present. he nears,

shares bright hellos and false surprise,
the clichés of 'how longs it been',
the mental notes, and 'fancy seeing
you', as interest loiters, dies,

for even sentiment's asleep;
they're strangers passing in the park,
the binding words in bedroom dark
forgotten now; the time to weep

long passed. it all seems so unreal:
from love to pain to nothingness,
a poignant metamorphosis;
renewal's edict not to feel

too much. reciting children's names
and ages, they resist the fancy
to confer on shared posterity,
or even love's immortal claims.

excusing, he departs, is keen
to get away, uneasy witness
to her old and tattered dress,
a sadder sight he's rarely seen.

she muses as he strides away,
of young man old or old man young,
and sighing, threads her way among
pinched feelings, pensive for a day.

Paternity

he'd come at last, his mother's plan
he visit this one grave, a man
he'd never known, dead in this land
of pastel leaves and wheaten grass
he fought in many years ago,
in one of history's futile stands.

the roses bud, and grounds are mown
where age-old trees have idly grown
among the acres of the dead,
a gesture to proclaim the lives
beneath sad rows of monoliths,
and bald inscriptions rarely read.

and there's the one; yet meagre words
stop short of adding what occurred:
a name, where 'fallen', though the date
confounds, unnerving him, for while
he's only forty and alive,
his father's dead at twenty-eight.

bemused, he kneels in fading light,
as feelings jostle for the right
to plead, his ordered life a lie:
his father now seems more alive,
a real and vital human being,
no faceless stranger passing by.

this man was slaughtered in his prime;
now years are out of kilter, time
has lost its natural place when
we as sons outlive our fathers:
just mere children who are fathers
still of plump and balding men.

a pluming bird sits on the grave
and warbles gently. breezes shave
the waving grass, and suddenly
it dawns that he alone devised
just who he's been; has never thought
about his lost paternity.

as lilac dims in twilight's sky,
he reaches out, still kneeling by
the grave, aware they're both alive;
and pensive, strokes the stone, a wall,
impermeable, that isolates him
from the meaning of his life.

he stands with newly won respect,
belatedly the new elect,
and in this land where soldiers ran
and fell, repeats the name aloud,
for what he was and has become,
is joined forever to this man.

Surreal

i don't know what i'm doing here, alone and mutinous,
a beachside suburb where the buses terminate.

i tumble from my nightmare ride, and find my feet,
as quilts of velvet black are hauled across a sky of aubergine,
and sudden milk bar brightness spills on asphalt streets
where mists of sand swirl round my feet.

i move towards a sea that heaves, soughing and primordial,
past fresh cat pee and fried potato fumes,
the 'to let' sign that swings askew on rusty hooks
to give cockeyed permission to the glistening drool
of snails on cracked cement.

two girls pass by in heels that stretch their lambent legs,
and swing their breasts, observe reaction, snigger, laugh.

the wind selects a mighty fig that with its patience tested,
claps its ample leaves defiantly,
while several dogs annoy the sun-less grass
that struggles to survive.

a startled woman shies at my approach, avoids my eyes,
and with her small divining torch,
is swallowed by the night.

i step on clammy sand that's even malleable to wills
less resolute than mine,
bypass a sleeping form concealed by cardboard sheets,
save for a hairy hand around an amber glass
that for a moment's flared by meddling moonlight
on its nowhere path across the oily waves.

then from the road a woman's screaming dislocates the quiet,
shrill voices vie in anger, lights come on,
and people mill around to pick allegiances.

it is no different here, this place of dreams,
a sun-adoring Mecca, capital of outdoor coffee and croissants,
and longed-for rendezvous;

behind the windows scoured in light, the darkness lurks:
spent marriages lie comatose in bed,
and reputations crumble over tea and toast;
the sanctimonious still thrill to virtue lost in halls of power,
and people eke out private grief.
i don't know what i'm doing here.

Dementia

as firm confederates they would tease
and laugh, disputing who was boss,
yet now the mantle's all her own
and he complies without demur,
as long as he can work out how.

she chatters as he stares ahead,
and cuts his toast in easy bites,
then with his early morning shave
she dabs some lather on his nose
to nurse the pretence of a joke.

and after lukewarm morning tea
in half-full double-handled mug,
she wipes the leavings from his mouth,
and fetches bleach to clean the shower
from not so savoury accident.

their ritual walk is therapy
beside the dusk's long-fingered shade,
his walker steered with shuffling gait,
dogged grimace stencilled on his face,
and she with gentle guiding hand.

she holds him fondly in their bed
and feels his unresponsive warmth,
as memories for a trice alight,
and zigzag off like butterflies:
the looks, the words, forgotten touch.

well-meaning others intervene,
revealing options she might take;
'no romance novel this,' she says,
'well camouflaged for you perhaps,
but what real love is all about.'

Unity

no pity in the mirror's grimace back,
revealing nothing of this grave attack
on life; his wish that he be snatched away,
in small part granted; not the ideal way
to cancel every debt; a month to wind
things up, or down, to hone the addled mind
and focus every lens, to see the rhyme
and reason when he shakes the hand of time.

then something fluttered, loitered softly on his shoulder,
wouldn't go away. was this the rumoured holder
of a secret that conferred a quiet completeness
on a life. the once pragmatic man bore witness:
power and rank now last in line, a scolded child;
the rock of hatred shattered; pride no more beguiled;
life's players entered, some to play their clumsy parts,
their burlesque unconvincing, dross of empty hearts;
and in the dying light his mind soon realised,
that what he understood could never be despised,

like time does not betray the unity of life and death,
for both are part of one design, so with resurgent breath
gives thanks for ruddy babes and workers' toil, for all romancing
lovers, and the dew that glistens on a web, for dancing
motes in shafts of light; and when his final moment's come,
says i'm the magpie's song, the jasmine's scent, i am the sun.

Twilight

lights come on. the twilight's come
and tensions of the day are done
for us, but not so for the man
who frames my window's worldly gaze

whose beachside treading howls a grief
his fraught escape gives no relief,
the burden of his heavy world
imprinted in the soulless sand

where silver flakes peel from the sea
and flagellate. immensity
of torment's goaded by the wave's
acidic licking of his wounds

to make him fall upon his knees
in supplication – prayers to please
the Gods, or is it something else
that he entreats. i cannot tell.

you're looking out she says, much more,
or should i say beyond, for
you're out there somewhere, not here,
so what's this thing you hope to find.

if she were privy to the way
he hauls his grief, she'd surely say
with stock cliché as dull as waves,
it's simply life's rich tapestry.

i could explain just what i see,
event and image faithfully,
but feeling's mix defies an honest
sense. it's my reality.

the rubbish must be taken out
she says, and if there's any doubt
about the car she says, i need
the four-wheel drive to take the kids.

my flattened palm's against the pane
in sad salute. as twilight wanes
he's leaving, hasn't seen, and darkness
hides the density of pain.

Son

we share those rapt and private things
my father dared not share with me,
the feelings culture and an age
permit between a son and father,
comforts now in souls laid bare.

the lake is oiled by dusk, relaxing
as the sun departs; the restaurant's
lyric ambience now smiling
on my sentiment; our 'catch-up'
melting into recollections

of the past: your awesome birth,
all crimped hot pink, the sweet milk smell;
your squat legs firming through the years
to speed you to blue ribbon feats
on many a stage. you're thirty now,

and underneath a violet sky
with spate of cheerful stars, we reach
across the bleak divide of time
and generations, tentative
till blood and empathy assert.

your manly frame was pliant once,
the blue inquiring eyes up-staring
from the table; smiling, gurgling,
helpless in consent; my fingers
slick with ochre excrement.

this lasting image makes me think
of all our loves, an allegory:
the giving selflessly with care,
and bared of all pretence, contentment
in the shared humilities.

Comedian

all florid with good cheer,
he knows they're captive now,
those looks of expectation,
senses honed for mirth
and minds agog to laugh at him,
at all his fabled escapades,
and other people's tragedies.
omnipotent,
he struts the stage,
and having seen it all before,
he reads them like a script:
full-throated laughter from the predisposed;
the prudish women thrilling to the bawdiness
with failing pretence of restraint;
the deaf and puzzled chuckling,
needing irony explained;
and even rare hyena laughs
that feed hilarity.

the dressing room's unearthly quiet,
and heavy with a loneliness;
the mirror-bordered lights
glare from their naked globes
to blench a sombre face;
the crumpled tissues open on the bench
like muddied flowers,
detritus of a glory newly past
already lost in time;
and muffled laughter spasms distantly.

alone
in hotel's terry towelling robe,
with brandy clinking in a seasoned hand,
he stares at city lights infinities below
that fizz in garish oranges and limes,
and contemplates his other life
that comedy's detached
from all that's real,
the way a world protects itself
with ammunition's laugh,
and moving to the sliding door
that opens on the darkness
all around,
he lifts his empty glass in mock salute
and laughs aloud,
the very public face
of private pain.

Rhea

a blush reveals horizon's sigh
to end the day; against coal sky
the church is etched in silhouette;
its lichened towers imposing, dark
forerunners of approaching cold
that bitter winter winds abet.

the gravestones, upright and askew,
accord the dead their meagre due,
at least for those with recency
or prideful with a wilting rose;
the others smoothed by needling rain,
are bare with lost posterity.

not treading on the faces cast
in earth, i read the epitaphs,
or listen as they speak to me,
surprised to see her kneeling down
with shears and trowel beside a grave
of miserly chronology,

and curious at such a sight,
for witches pillage graves at night,
and not a girl with ready smile
called Rhea, standing for my name,
extending me her fine-boned hand
with unsophisticated style.

he's not a relative she says,
for Cedric Jones has long been dead;
the choking weeds and crumbling stone
need care; it's just so peaceful here,
and all the dead deserve respect,
a gesture i have made my own.

we chat until the darkness spreads,
our audience the knowing dead,
for who could fathom any more
the slings and arrows that we bear,
and cede perspective silently,
than those who've lived it all before.

the wind soughs round the towering stone,
recycling, chilling to the bone;
as fetching tools, i help her stand,
and with the usual pleasantries,
she leaves in haste, though for a tender
moment, holds, not shakes my hand.

and for a while i linger there;
though night is gelid, black and bare
of stars, i know no urgency
to leave; have never felt this way
before; a balance and a peace
of life and death in harmony.

School

images cavort and come to rest,
attach themselves to names,
gold letters on the honour board
that dull with subjugated time;
the ghosts of ages past
now prey on kindled sentiment,
to haunt grandparents' day;

why this need then to profess
the swim of lapsing years,
admit a mite of ownership
with all who come here now:
'i was a student once,
and in this very room',
still feel its timeless legacy,
my life's domesticated tutelage;

she'll look at me indulgently and smile,
an older man's nostalgia commonplace,
so what else can she say,

but please feel free,
and so i stoop beneath the mobiles
and the artwork pegged on lines of string;
the panoply of richly laminated aids
defies routine austerity.

a pealing somewhere;
must be Susie Parker with the heavy bell
she gathers from the office
several times a day,
and wields with both her little hands
like Rustum's sword;
it's time for bottled recess milk
still warming in the crates,
yet drinkable if Stevie Dowd has stopped
the magpies pecking at the tinfoil tops,
especially those of blue;
ink monitor today, it's time for me
to fill the desk wells,
check the pen nibs aren't all bent,
report new scarrings in the wood
like Ronnie's carving of a penis
on Giuseppe's desk.

another bell;
it's time to come back in,
so why's he tugging at my sleeve
with 'grandpa, pa';
'hang on a second, mate', i'm curt,
'i have to find my flute
to help the children march back into class,
and George is waiting with the old bass drum,
so skip out there and ask him
if it's "British Grenadiers"
or "Do Ye Ken John Peel".'

Reaction

approaching
        shirt awry   and pulled from trousers
by a simian gait   or just the constant
swaying
that he can't control
                        he's independent
                moving forward
even with the leg that capers
like a hose not held.

you're staring she admonishes   unwrapping peanut slice
while i with steady hand   and fingers that obey   that flex
and work together   pour the tea.
of course you're not   i want to bark   there's something wrong
with everything i do   yet as the pain of separation's   bad
enough   i opt for silence   and decide to let the tension drain
perhaps in time to disappear   restoring what we used to have.

                hello
he rasps stentorian   beneath the beanie
        pulled to meet his eyes   set deep
and close
                        inside a pinched yet not unsightly face
i'm   going   for   a   walk
his pride goes charging through the phlegmy drawl
                        a beaming pleasure   and a flap of hands.

i watch him go   and stand   to feel the flowing strength
intoxicated   by my robustness   the spine so straight   and
arms and legs   that spring unthinking   blooded into life
and feel uneasiness   a shame   that's little tempered by relief
at being whole.

thus sobered by reflection,
i avoid the stock cliché
about the grace of god,
and turning to embrace the sun,
to draw good fortune
from the glitter-sprinkled lake,
i sense her yielding presence
by my side,
and feel the message
of her hand.

Age

to 'come of age' is eighteen now,
so where does that leave us;
perhaps for 'age'
a qualifier might suffice,
like 'old',
or better still 'mature',
a euphemism lacing it with common sense,
a fruitfulness
like bordeaux mellowing in oak,

an age when sport and sex and politics
are relegated
to a grudging second place,
as escalating stories do the rounds
to meet with incredulity,
perhaps despondent nod,
yet always trumped
by limitless mortality:
'it's in the bowel and terminal,
a month or two at best,
not forty yet
and three kids under ten.'

the list of truants grow
at school reunions,
named yet never shamed,
their foibles lamely glorified,
while some attempt
to recollect a face by classroom seat,
as kindled folklore turns to ash.

still others count the liver spots
or strangled dried-up blood,
devour their cache of pills,
acquire a bike,
or wear a broad-brimmed hat;
and several in their all too early
waking hours
can feel the evil tenderness
that shifts and loiters deep within,
and bides its time to pounce,

all adamant beyond a doubt,
they've come of age.

Wally

just went upstairs to sleep
one summer's afternoon
and never did wake up,
his six and fifty years
imprinted on a rugose face,
and raison d'etre
the world had commandeered;
his bonhomie sustained by drink,
a signature
the contract of a life expunged.

behind the masquerade
were hints of bitter family truths,
the day-long aftermath
of too much beer
in night time bitterness
and early morning petulance
that mocked his public cheer,
made victims in his sacred home.

so where's the fabled line in sand
that marks 'enough'
defining harmful ways;
what private history mitigates a crime;
is there a perpetrator's state of mind
excusing hurt,
and what price must we all indulge
for charity.

i used my internet and did research
on Changi, Sandarkan;
unspoken horrors with their hidden scars
that might have launched his flight
from all privation
to a drunken thirst
that never could be quenched,
a voluntary insanity;
perhaps he felt he had to live
his own domesticated Changi,
mere survival forfeiting the right
to lasting peace.

Transience

my heart like yours is stale and tired
of passion; what we once desired
has gone to sleep, so let's enjoy
the final moments we can share.

your eyes betray the emptiness
of knowing time will never bless
us with the prodigality
we knew, and thrill of that first kiss.

we'll amble through the park she said,
indulge our memories instead
of moping here about the past,
or dwelling on what might have been.

the canopy of trees above
subdues all talk of mislaid love,
and friendly sun that frets to jewel
her hair, seems very far away.

she gambols, stooping suddenly
to scoop up leaves beneath a tree,
the crisp autumnal browns and golds
all clotted damp with early dew,

and running with them in her arms
a wood nymph with her mystic charms,
she sings the music of the trees,
and laughing, showers them over me.

yet rapture turns to deathly quiet,
as gloomy in that filtered light,
we hold each other guardedly
in final epicene embrace.

we've lingered where the angels tread,
i'm just so sad it's gone she said;
will other loves exist for us,
or are our hearts too old and tired.

as love must surely vanquish all,
we can but answer to its call,
and hope that if it smiles on us,
it perseveres in lasting flame

Death

they say the comatose can hear
your every word when edging near
to death; just talk the nurses say,
profess your love, seek absolution,
simply tell them you'll be fine,
or if you feel inclined, then pray.

it's early hours. blear lights outside
are waning; all is dark; beside
the bed, a makeshift couch for me
to watch her, hear the stertorous breath
rasp life from laden air, mouth open,
jaw unhinged: time's cautery.

it must be what my Catholic friends
feel at confession: words that mend
the broken bridges, rare, defined
by place, and easy to relate
because there are no trials to bear,
no seeing eyes to read the mind.

deep in the cache of memory,
the images are odd; i see
her tennis serve, the way she'd tell
her yarns, the morning tea with cake;
and prattling to her, voiceless, blind,
consider life as consequential.

2 a.m. her grating stops.
no need to rush, i move across
to verify; she's now at peace;
for me, no grief, just emptiness:
the memory of lost worlds, and blueprint
for our earthly show's decease.

i interrupt the nurses chatter
with the news, indulge their patter,
brush one final kiss that's cold
on sterile skin, retreat in to
the night, relieved, confronted, sad
my testament remains untold.

my drive home's blushed by amber stars
from streetlights, yet she isn't far
away, the brief ubiquity
that's granted when we kiss the lips
of time; our talk's revealing now,
unchecked by life's captivity.

Prospect

as waking stars were blinking
through drapes of surging cloud
a brief parturient quiet
divined what he avowed

i'll always love you dearest
till all the seas run dry
and every blazing star
drops from the hallowed sky

till fish and birds are soul mates
when streams and mountains speak
till sun heats up the ocean
and all the planets meet

your beauty is my orbit
the lover's gift we share
for all it takes to charm me
is a single auburn hair

and time will make no difference
our love's immortal key
will keep us locked together
for all eternity

but time's a bitter critic
she parried with denial
it creases withers scars
and growls when you might smile

time has its way with beauty
what charms you now must fade
ephemeral's not eternal
and debits must be paid

though love's a chaste flower now
ambrosial and fine
it too will fall beneath
the noiseless foot of time

as scudding clouds raced on
indifferent to his slight
a billion winking stars
laughed long in to the night

Uncle

i'm here yet somehow not,
belonging and remote,
a servant of my different lives:
the one of yesteryear,
and one i'm living now,
both tethered by a thin chronology.

perhaps he feels these iterations too,
his face now reddened by the blood
that threatens to ignite,
and hearing aids that fail to tamp
the white extruding hair.

we sit together,
lineage conferring empathy,
or just our history,
and the Damoclean sword.

the last of five,
it needs no literacy to read his thoughts
that hover,
settle on the coffin and alight,
to guess at time.

struck matches in the dark,
he snatches at a date,
a phrase an incident,
the incandescence dying,
left behind by jumbled thoughts
that roam across the years,
the eulogy a bald chronology
that leaves her anchored on a pin,
exhibit with generic Latin tag,
revealing nothing of her flame of love
or smell of fear;
if only he could sift the clichés,
rip the words apart,
expose the very pith of her;
confront the unction of the priest
who dampens earthly sentiment,
belittling self for promises of life beyond.

so difficult to drive these days,
he won't come to the wake
where tea with cake
and chastened gentleness
are tokens of placating death.

Theatre

on Shakespeare's stage of life, performances are rare
with only seven parts to play,
the exits and the entrances that span our time
from puking infant to the slippered pantaloon.

and yet contemporary impresarios are told
by seasoned thespians
that they'll play any role at any time,
be anything the action might demand,
for actors in particular they say,
are several different people after all;
implying that they lack unique identity,
and can't portray their one inherent script,
but rather glory in their triumphs
like chameleons that change their colour to disguise,
perhaps protest against the anguish of a life.

beyond the theatre's stage the daily matinees endure:
small children with their prompted lines,
the adolescents aping roles of want-to-be sophisticates,
celebrities affecting to assume the world,
and tossing off her heels
the partygoer wondering how the audience received
her night's interpretation of congeniality;

all looking for a singularity and self
that's forged from remnants
of a childhood and experience,
and from a painful inner questioning
beyond the plaudits of soliloquies,
a oneness some will never know,
that Hamlets and Othellos
only grasp when action's done,
and others find when plots confound,
and in traditions of Greek drama
gods appear on stage.

Regret

i feel there's no such thing as chance,
that nothing's random in this world;
to find him on the beach at dusk
with damask sky and citrus moon,
the faintest pencilling of cloud
that interwove our scribbled names
to augur something heaven-sent,
the ocean silently benign
allowing words to penetrate
our souls, and eyes reveal, confirm.

it's everything a poet craves,
this splendid castle in the air,
a mind's invention and retreat,
for single fantasies transform
a million harsh realities;
i must have felt forlorn, alone,
perhaps the evening sky was louring,
i was cold, and he like me
in search of human antidote,
beneath a sky that swallows stars.

don't look at me with pitying eyes,
it's over thirty years ago,
and while i've wondered where he is
or if he's lost a partner too;
your father gave me everything
a woman has the right to claim:
fidelity and certainty,
and not ephemeral star-crossed lovers
blind to adolescent follies
they most certainly commit.

and yet a shadow falls on age
to usher in unwelcome doubt,
for i renounced the greatest passion
that i ever knew, mistrust
of love, or was it of myself:
the feeling that i wasn't worthy,
destined for a prosaic world;
if our beliefs mean everything,
then shouldn't love be sacred too,
made into something beautiful.

Time

beyond the muddled sticks and frames,
a motley brotherhood is propped,
their faces vacuous as fallow
fields, or settled in assent.
the television mutes false cheer,

yet no one looks. their images
are private ones with more repeats
than *Fawlty Towers*. so do they think
wives back into this bankrupt room,
for faces are unreadable

in every lucent mauve-veined head.
if watched clocks never move, then time
is squandered here, unchecked in breakneck
flight by ticking hands that shadow
lives against eternity.

what lurks beyond the vacant looks;
do words forget to shape themselves,
lost in the jumble of a mind,
a crumbling partnership with thought,
to leave them inarticulate;

or have they seen it all before,
so enter time beyond all words
where thoughts are finite after all,
and nothing's left for them to know
or feel, so nothing need be said.

all bonhomie, the nurse comes in
with tea, and dodges walking frames;
'time flies' i offer emptily,
ashamed at once of seeming trite;
'but surely time stands still,' she says

surprised, 'and we're the ones who fly.'
arthritic fingers claw at mugs,
and with their backs turned on the future,
watch time's present rush away
to inundate a cluttered past.

Schadenfreude

a teacher in the local primary school,
Bettina was disgusted, thought it cruel

that she earned little kudos, certain test
of worth, for she was better than the rest

of them; 'the years of teaching's made them stale,
all mediocre, dull, beyond the pale'

she'd say to each, and 'confidentially',
'the only good ones here are you and me',

and hating praise for them, could not abide
their recognised success, though justified;

if colleagues were affirmed, then woe betide,
the mad dog's teeth bit deep, and something died

in her; yet craving praise she'd gravitate
to bosom friendships she'd manipulate

and safeguard jealously; with gifts she built
relationships, massaged to kindle guilt

by venting hurt at their alleged neglect,
and seeking sympathy from deep regret;

she'd relish other's pain, for then she'd comfort
them, insinuate, and so she sought

affliction, giving solace to attest
the void that filled her own unhappiness,

uniting them, she hoped, as intimates,
but there's the catch; another's pain awaits

a cause, so she began creating it
through made-up stories, gossip, lies, to wit,

until her trusting target felt the pain,
and she was there to empathise again,

yet those with joie de vivre, and light of heart
would make her ugly, setting her apart.

this world's awry, and hers a dangerous game:
another's pain her joy; their joy her pain.

Visit

there's tight security among
the scented gums; no willing passage
from this cushioned world and doubtful
cheer of regulation meals,
assisted showers and toileting.

what feelings must have tortured her
to see their loving fifty years
of partnership reduced to wards
of four; just bring a change of clothes
they said, pyjamas, toiletries.

my first time here's congenial,
accosted by the manager,
solicitous, and showing me
the room with 'let me know if we
can help', before he strides away.

my father's tilted in the bed,
and staring fixedly ahead;
the crumbs about his mouth attest
to tea and biscuits, standard fare
before lunch sandwiches and fruit.

across the room an old man rocks,
another snores; and here consigned,
my father must eke out his twilight
days, this man who loved and guided,
king within his sacred realm.

'i think i'll like it here' he whispers,
barely audible; my raw heart
lurches, tenderness i've never
felt awash, and new regret
for all things past i could have done.

i pick my way through broken lives,
inertia, empty looks and anguished
calls, the wandering naked relic;
now my father's surreal world
that mocks the code of sanity.

'please thank the manager' i tell
the nurse. 'he isn't here today,'
she laughs at my surprise, 'our Ted
is just another patient here,
he used to be the mayor of Ryde.'

Introspection

our neighbour Frank, who ridiculed
the ancients' damning of the unexamined life,
declaring it was simply Greek to him,
that he knew who he was, thanks very much,
that 'thinking doesn't make it so,'
met with an accident:
a four-wheel driver sent him to the hospital
to nurse his wounds
and months of introspection,
traction for his primitive philosophy;

yet asked what he had learned about himself
from healing time,
what insights flowed from thought
and gnawing pain,
affected incredulity: 'so what's to learn,'
and mocked his questioner with parody:
'when i discover who i am,
i'll finally be free,'
and then more acidly,
'as if i don't know after all!.'

he died wide-eyed, out-staring, no surprise.

pristine and Omo-white White Ladies,
tasteful with maroon relief,
adorned the church,
and fraying knots of mourners thought
of washing on the line
and picking children up from school;
for Frank,
the thought of what came next
had neither daunted nor intrigued,
no question of a purpose for his years,
or just deserts,
not even dying visions
of the thump of dirt on wood,
and trenchant lettered stone;
nor had he ever wondered at the meaning
of the universe,
sussed-out a place to call his own
beneath a blue insinuating sky
or brilliant swarm of evening stars.

Egocentrism

the ward was full of women
stoically bearing pain
yet from a door-side bed
'i won't come here again

this food just can't be eaten
it's sodden mash' she whined
'you ask so much in charges
i should be wined and dined

it took at least an hour
to finally get a bed
and every doctor busy
with someone else instead

blind freddy knows i'm hurting
it can't be that unclear
i should be checked each hour
but no one's even near'

'some women here are dying'
the duty nurse declared
'and your infected toe
can hardly be compared

bed two has emphysema
bed one a heart that's weak
three's chemo isn't working
so think before you speak'

and even as she countered
a beeping shrilled the day
and nurses came from nowhere
response without delay

'it's cardiac arrest
Miss Browne in number one'
a trolley soon appeared
with doctors on the run

'an angioplasty, nurse'
a grim-faced doctor sighed
so give her heparin now
until she's stabilised

but as they wheeled away
and down the corridor
the piercing sound flatlined
no beeping like before

the voices reached crescendo
the trolley raced apace
to leave the ward behind
a funereal place

and in the deathly hush
where Miss Browne used to be
a strident voice bawled out
'has no one thought of me'

Exit

as summer brilliance cools to bronze
and autumn tangerine has paled
when winter hoar is on the ground
my time's no more

so do not be distraught for me
my time to live and die is gone
and gentle spring will bud for you
with new-found joy

i've savoured what the world affords
to know its pleasures and its pain
so do not grieve that i have gone
or not lived well

in giving in extremis thanks
for all the riches of my life
your friendship and solicitude
have been my all

the boast of eminence and power
were courted in brief interludes
yet searching for less fleeting truths
i found love's boon

i have no claims of special worth
nor make humility a show
for public censure of myself
is feigned self-praise

whatever words you speak today
remember if they resonate
a thousand voices tease the truth
that limns each life

no longer scenes of eucalypts
or scented fires that warm the heart
i'm summonsed to another place
where souls can dwell

perhaps in salad green of day
or lucid hush before a storm
you'll sense my presence in the air
and sigh my name

as summer brilliance cools to bronze
and autumn tangerine has paled
if winter hoar has long since gone
then spring must come

www.ingramcontent.com/pod-product-compliance
Lightning Source LLC
Chambersburg PA
CBHW071449080526
44587CB00014B/2045